Become a First Style Fashionista!

A girl's guide to ultimate fabulosity

By Beth Newman

newmanimage.info
beth@newmanimage.com

Praise for "Become a First Style Fashionista" and Beth Newman

Image Consultant and Life Coach Beth Newman has written a fun new book called **Become a First Style Fashionista.** This gem of a book is packed with nuggets of wisdom geared towards increasing the confidence and self awareness of middle school girls. Whether it's etiquette, wardrobe analysis, fashion tips, or success strategies you are interested in, this book covers it all. Beth will assist you in becoming the best "you" that you can be!
-Cari L. Murphy
Best-Selling Author/Broadcaster
Host of the "Create Change Now" Radio Show
http://www.CreateChangeNowRadio.com
Get Cari's Latest Book: www.CreateChangeNow.com

Beth Newman's book, **Become a First Style Fashionista**, is an excellent resource for young women. In a fun, conversational manner, Beth delivers excellent etiquette and style tips while also providing inspirational, thought-provoking quotes and fun, yet informative quizzes. Become a First Style Fashionista is a must-have for all girls and would be an excellent tool in any middle school classroom as well!
-Vanessa Dyne, Middle School English/Language Arts Instructor, The Honor Roll School

Beth Newman clearly has what it takes to survive the journey from the awkward pre-teen years to becoming a confident, poised, and successful woman.
-Becky Mason, mom of First Style Fashionista, Lauren

Enjoyable and humorous, yet so real and beneficial, as it provides guidance for girls to overcome their awkward pre-teen years into becoming confident, well-mannered, and chic young women. This book provides fabulous advice and tips every girl can definitely use! Thanks, Miss Beth!
-Zainab, First Style Fashionista

Acknowledgements

I'd like to dedicate this book to my late father, Ron Miller. Although he didn't understand me at times (and goodness knows, he tried!), he always encouraged me to strive for my personal best, and most importantly, to be happy. And that, my darlings, is what it's all about!

This book could not be possible without the help of some truly fabulous people. Words cannot express how much I appreciate you all for your support, encouragement, advice, and love over the years! I must, therefore, give shout-outs to:

My husband, Kent Newman, who does all the work behind the scenes for Newman Image – you rock, literally, and I couldn't make it without you!

Tish and Malcolm Wolter
Irene Miller
Billye and Larry Newman
Laura Pennino
The Honor Roll School
Chic Galleria Publications
Focus on Women Magazine

First Style Fashionista Models

You'll see photos of truly amazing young women throughout this book. Each of them represents what a First Style Fashionista is: confident, poised, kind, and compassionate. Each of them is devoted to being the absolute best she can be, in every area of her life.

This book is full of scenarios that reveal 'what not to do'; please know that each girl represented on the pages always, without fail, exemplifies 'what to do'. These young women are the best of the best, and in no way represent any behavior that is counter to that of a First Style Fashionista.

On that note, I must take this opportunity to thank the parents of my First Style Fashionista Models:

Marnee & Brett Axelson
Casey DeShazo
Maureen Dondero
Tammy Higginbothem
Tina & Randall Houston
Lynn Johnson
Rene LeBlanc
Tasha & David Lynch
Sonja & Scott Madigan
Becky & David Mason
Kelly Noel
Cheryl North
Tianna Patterson
Laura & Jim Rough
Annette Robison
Becky & Ron Russell
Mark Russell
Beth & Dustin Smith
Melissa Terrill
Jennifer & Eddie Valadez
Kay Wade

Additional photos provided by Pathathai Chunavam, Jason Stitt, and Jamie Williams of www.dreamstime. com.

Table des métiers

(Table of contents...yes, you will get a little French lesson here, too!)

Page 65
Bonus:
Your 52-Weeks of Fabulosity
Journal!

Your opportunity to write down your goals, dreams, and anything else that will help you as you travel the road to fabulosity!

Introduction

What is First Style?

First Style promotes 'the total package'. Geared toward pre-teens and teens, First Style provides them with valuable knowledge and success strategies that will empower them for the rest of their lives.

Fashion is one of those areas. We live in an age in which 'anything goes', wardrobe-wise, for students and for adults. How we present ourselves to the world is vitally important. Like it or not, we are judged by the clothing on our backs and the way in which we groom ourselves. Appropriateness is key here, and that's why fashion plays a tremendous role in the First Style curriculum. Fashion should be fun, and should represent who a girl is – we're all wired differently, and one girl's fashion preferences may not be those of her best friend. That's okay, and that's the beauty of fashion – it's a means by which we can express ourselves and who we are!

First Style promotes good manners. Graduates of the First Style program come away from the experience confident in knowing what to do in any given social situation. They understand that our actions have results. The 'mean-girl' phenomena currently sweeping our society is cause for alarm, and First Style girls learn why this trend is dangerous and just plain wrong. First Style teaches compassion, empathy, and reminds us all of the importance of The Golden Rule.

Another area that First Style girls come to understand is that we won't look our best if we don't feel our best. Healthy eating and exercise tips are an integral part of the First Style program. Discussions on the dangers of eating disorders and other unhealthy behaviors are also touched upon. It is my sincerest wish that each First Style girl learns the value of good health, and adopts its practices at an early age.

Success strategies, too, play a huge role in the First Style program. I share with the girls tips on goal-setting, organization, positive self-talk, and visualization.

My mission through First Style is to assist every girl dealing with what can be those 'awkward middle school years' to develop confidence in each aspect of her life. The habits she forms now will most likely follow her into adulthood. It's not a cookie-cutter program that insists she do 'exactly as I say'; this program , designed with a 'total package' approach in mind, will empower her and encourage her to strive for her personal best in all that she does.

Every young woman deserves an opportunity to be the absolute best she can be!

For more information about First Style, feel free to visit www.newmanimage.info or www.firststyle.webs.com. I also cordially invite you to become a First Style Fashionista on Facebook!

Premiere Partie: Lights, Camera, Fashion!

**"How you dress tells the world how you expect to
be treated"**
-Clinton Kelly

And that's oh-so-true, my darlings. Too often, even
grown-ups don't consider the importance of the clothing they wear. That's why it's our job – yours and
mine – to set the fashion example for others. Let's
help get our society 'spiffied up!'

But before we do, let's consider where we are...

Style Status Quiz

1. **How often to you buy new clothes to rev up your wardrobe?**

a. Every month, as fashions change

b. Every 3-4 months, as seasons change

c. Once a year, when the annual sales are going on

d. Uh...what?

2. **What does your wardrobe mainly consist of?**

a. Nothing but brand names

b. A variety things; not necessarily brand names, but they're nice

c. Sweats and flip-flops

d. What's a wardrobe?

3. My accessories are

a. Top of the line and very expensive

b. A nice necklace my grandmother gave me and a few things I picked up at the mall

c. Stuff my older sister gave me that she didn't want anymore

d. Accessories? Who cares?

4. When shoe shopping, what do you look for?

a. The expensive shoes I see in Mom's **Vogue** magazine

b. Cute shoes that are comfortable, like the ones I find at Old Navy or Forever 21

c. I don't shop for shoes until the one pair I wear are too small.

d. Cheap flip-flops I find at the local drugstore

5. You primarily shop at

a. Hollister, Abercrombie...places like that

b. Forever 21, Old Navy...places like that

c. Garage sales, my sister's closet...places like that

d. Shop? I just wear what people give me!

6. Your best friend is hosting a party. You...

a. Rush out and buy the coolest outfit you can find

b. Buy a new top and some earrings that go with a skirt you already own

c. Borrow a cool necklace from your sister to wear.

d. Wear exactly what you wear every day. Why bother getting something new?

Mostly A's:
You are beyond First Style Fashionista status! Your image as a fashionista is very important to you. You spare no expense when it comes to achieving your signature look! Be careful, though: don't brag about your name brands, and don't let them consume who you are.

Mostly B's:
You are a First Style Fashionista. You realize that fashion is important, but you also recognize the power of bargain shopping and making do with what you have. Well done!

Mostly C's:
You're just-this-close to being a First Style Fashionista. Sure, fashion can be fun, but it isn't the most important thing to you.

Mostly D's:
My dear! Although you're to be commended for your 'who cares?' attitude, the fact of the matter is that a lot of people care. What you wear says a lot about you. It's time for you to put some thought into your image.

Now, let's take a look at some of the issues that commonly face a First Style Fashionista:

Idol Chat

Sara's favorite celebrity is Mary McRockstar. Mary sings, dances, and stars in her own TV show. Because Mary McRockstar does, in fact, rock, Sara wants to be just like her. She envisions herself on stage in front of cheering crowds, of winning every award there is to win, and wearing those wonderfully tiny little outfits Mary wears...

Wait a minute.

Mary McRockstar is much older than Sara and has a right to wear those tiny little outfits. Sara is only 12. What works for Mary McRockstar is not going to work favorably for Sara.

Clothes send a message about us. If we dress appropriately for our age, that tells the world that we're confident and that we respect ourselves. If we copy what our scantily-clad idols are wearing, that also sends a message: that we've little self-respect and we'll go to certain lengths to get attention (trust me, my darlings, this is negative attention you'll be getting, and it could follow you around for a long time.) Copying someone never works.

The great Judy Garland (you know, Dorothy from **The Wizard of Oz**) once said, "Why not be a first rate version of yourself rather than a second rate version of someone else?"

Who Cares?

Daisy hates to dress up. She prefers to wear old, oversized sweat pants and flip flops everywhere. Often, she'll wear the same shirt three days in a row. She simply isn't interested in fashion. Her mother buys her nice things to wear, but Daisy feels that it's what's on the inside that matters. Daisy's right....to a degree.

What we carry on the inside – things like kindness, generosity, empathy, respect – are far more important that the clothes on our backs. However, we can better relay our wonderful traits if our outward appearance is at its best. It's hard to set a good example if your clothes just aren't working for you. We live in a visual society. Think about it: how does your favorite teacher measure up physically compared to your least favorite teacher? Most likely, your fave favors a sleek, put-together look while in the classroom.

Remember, what we choose to wear tells the world an awful lot about us. Let your wardrobe positively reflect the oh-so-fabulous you!

Throw a Fit

Call Carrie confused. One day, she was an ordinary girl whose clothes fit her just fine. The next day, things started sprouting and blooming and...well, you know what's going on. Instead of seeking out some new clothes, Carrie tried her best to wear what she'd been wearing all along. Her jeans fit so tightly she could barley zip them, her buttons on her shirt cried, "Help me!", and her skirts could easily pass for a mere ruffle that barely covers her rear-end.

Call Poppy perplexed. She's already gone through the blooming and sprouting phase that Carrie's dealing with right now. Poppy's problem, however, is that she's lost a great deal of what her mom affectionately called her 'baby-fat'. Even though she's only in 8th grade, her friends say she could pass for a grown woman. Poppy feels self-conscious, though, and continues to wear her baby-fat phase clothes, even though they fit like a tent. What's a girl to do?

First of all, both girls need to accept the changes in their bodies. It's part of growing up, and we all have to deal with it. There's no shame in becoming a woman. Secondly, they must recognize that proper fit will always flatter. Too-tight clothes look and feel uncomfortable, and may lead people to think certain things about you (go back and review what we told Sara). Too-big clothes give the appearance that you simply don't care (go back and review what we told Daisy).

No one can be stylish if her clothes don't fit well. Love your body and embrace what's happening to it. Celebrate it with a wonderful wardrobe – you deserve it!

Baby Talk

Jane's parents drive her crazy! Even though she's in seventh grade, her mom and dad still pick out her clothes for her. She has absolutely no say in what she wears. The worst part is that the clothes they get her are similar to the ones she wore in fourth grade. It's frustrating and so embarrassing! All of her other friends get to choose what they wear. What's Jane to do – she feels hopeless!

The hardest thing for any parent is the realization that their child is growing up. Jane should have a mature conversation with her parents about her dilemma.

"Mom, Dad, there's something important I need to speak with you about," says Jane.

"Of course," they reply, "go ahead."

Jane sits down calmly, her posture good and straight, and looks them in the eye.

"I feel I'm old enough now to pick out my own clothes. I'm in seventh grade now. I work hard to make good grades, I stay out of trouble, and I do all my chores. I'd really appreciate the opportunity to wear what I want to wear," Jane remains calm during her opening statement. She doesn't whine, and keeps her voice low yet cheery.

"Well, Janie," her mom begins, "so much out there for girls your age just isn't appropriate."

"I know, Mom, but I've done my homework, and I've found some really cute outfits that I think you'll like for me." Jane pulls out copies of **Teen Vogue** and **American Girl** and shows her parents that age-appropriate outfits do exist. They agreed to let her pick her own clothes, provided they get final approval. "You guys are awesome!" Jane proclaimed. "Thank you so much!"

Jane won this battle for two reasons: she handled the situation maturely and had done some research to support her request. Additionally, she scores big points for remembering to thank her parents for giving her a chance.

Maturity and consistently doing the right thing go a long way with parents. Keep that in mind.

No Money, No Funny

Ali's dad got fired from his job, so money's even scarcer in their household than ever before. Ali's in 8th grade and absolutely loves clothes. She spends hours in the library looking through fashion magazines, wishing she could have the latest styles. There simply isn't any extra money for anything other than essentials, though. Some of the kids at school have noticed her tattered jeans and worn-out shoes, and they give her a hard time about them. In her dreams, Ali's a fashionista. In real life, she's anything but, and she gets so sad about her lack of style that she breaks down and cries.

Ali's situation rings true for many girls, but there is hope. Ali could earn a little extra money doing odd jobs for neighbors (babysitting, raking leaves, light house-cleaning, or tutoring a younger student, for example). She could also take a cue from a wonderful old movie called **Pretty In Pink**. In the movie, Andi, a poor girl in love with a rich boy, makes her own clothes, including her prom dress. Was she dressed exactly like the other girls in her school? No, and that's what made her look even more fabulous – no one else was wearing what she wore! She had no problem accepting old clothes from the woman she worked for in a music store, either. She altered them into some amazing works of wearable art! And best of all, two boys fell in love with her – enough said.

Don't let lack of money get you down or kill your style dreams. With a little imagination and work, you can make them come true!

Problems Solved...Now, Where to Start?

A true First Style Fashionista does her homework. She notices what the celebrities are wearing on television and in movies. She studies age-appropriate fashion magazines and determines what's best for her. She takes Mom or another trusted adult along on a shopping spree and is open to their honest opinions.

Fashion is a fantastic way to express ourselves, and to let others know who we really are. It's vital, therefore, that we send the correct message about ourselves. Are you casually chic or more of a girly-girl? Sporty or studious? Funky or frilly? Maybe you're a little bit of everything, and that's okay. Fashion is about fun! The challenge is finding something that's trendy and age appropriate. No matter your own personal style, as long as you've got a few good basics, you're good to go.

Let's take it from the top:

Shirts and blouses can be form-fitting, but not skintight. They should not reveal any cleavage. Hide the bra straps.

Jeans and trousers should cover the behind entirely, even while sitting. Be sure the old rhyme "I saw London, I saw France...." doesn't apply to you. Keep your undergarments out of sight. Logos and phrases draw attention. Do you want everyone staring at your rear-end?

Skirts should fall at least one inch lower than the tip of your middle finger, especially those you wear to school or church.

Shoes can be tricky. It's easy to want to wear the same pair with every outfit, but we're at the age in which we need to break that habit. Low heels are okay, but only on special occasions. Flip-flops are only for super-casual outings (the beach, the mall, etc.).

It's extremely important that no matter the occasion or the outfit, we insure that our clothes are clean and wrinkle-free. Also, inspect your garments carefully to make sure that there are no stains, rips, or tears. If you don't already know how, learn to sew buttons and mend hems.

Consider taking an inventory of your closet. It's a good idea to sort through (and give away) the things you no longer wear. Jot down a list of items you'd like to incorporate.

Take advantage of the handy-dandy list below to take an accurate account:

Items I Need:

a.

b.

c

Items I Want:

a.

b.

c.

Items That Need Mending:

a.

b.

c.

Dazzle the Eyes...
Accessorize!

Accessories such as earrings, necklaces, and bracelets can make or break an outfit. These items are intended to complement your wardrobe. Some of the coolest accessories today are aimed at young women. Have fun here! However, remember the following (these are old rules, but they still hold true today):

Choose one or two accessories (a funky necklace and cool bracelet, perhaps) rather than covering yourself with jewelry. The idea is to spruce up your outfit and not to look like a Christmas tree.

Long, dangling earrings are best worn in the evening.

Hats are a super-great way to top off an outfit (they're also great for hiding a bad hair day!) Make sure hats are seasonally appropriate. You wouldn't wear one made of straw in the winter, nor would you wear heavy tweed in the summer.

Add-on's are those little special things that jazz up an outfit: a funky belt, a vest, scarves, etc. You'll find add-on's at every boutique – they're the smaller items located close to the register.

Helpful Hint

It's always a good idea to plan your outfit, including accessories, the night before. Here's a little checklist to help you remember what to include:

Date:
One the bottom:

One the top:

The add-on's:

The shoes:

The earrings:

The necklace:

The bag:

You can even lay out your clothing and accessories the night before – that saves you tons of time each morning!

Time to Make-Up

You've reached the age in which you may be toying with the idea of makeup. This is a decision you and your parents need to discuss. If they're okay with it, that's great, but make sure you keep it minimal at best.

Sixth and seventh grades: start small; a bit of blush, neutral-toned eye shadow, and some lip gloss is fine. As you move into eighth grade, you can experiment with concealer, foundation, and eyeliner. Of course, you can add a little more each year as you get older. Less is more for First Style Fashionistas.

Good, Clean Fun!

One simply can't be stylish if she's not clean. Shower daily, and use antiperspirant. Wash your hair as needed (some hair textures don't require daily washing; some do. If your hair feels gross, it probably is) and condition it each time. Brush your teeth. Clean your nails and don't walk around with chipped polish! Make sure that crusty eye stuff that forms in the corner of your eye during the night is gone before you leave the house in the morning.

Skin Care

You may be experiencing skin problems now: pimples, zits, whatever you want to call them...they're gross and can really ruin your day! There are plenty of products available for you. Should the over-the-counter stuff not work for you, ask your folks to take you to a dermatologist who can prescribe something for you. Do whatever you must to battle those blemishes!

Depending on your skin type, you'll benefit from a weekly facial. These can be done at home, and with things right out of the pantry:

Banana Mask for Oily Skin

Ingredients:
  1 banana, preferably ripe
  1 tbsp honey
  An orange or a lemon

Preparation:
Mix the banana and honey together.
Add a few drops of juice from an orange or a lemon.
Apply to face for 15 minutes before rinsing with a cool washcloth or a steaming warm washcloth.

Milk Mask for Dry Skin

Ingredients:
  1 tsp powdered milk
  1 tbsp runny honey
  1 tsp aloe vera gel
  2 drops essential oil

Mix ingredients well, apply to face, let sit for 15 minutes, wash off with warm water. This recipe is enough for two – loads of fun to do with a friend!

Rose Face Mask for Combinations Skin

This mask, based on roses, is perfect for balancing out the oily and dry areas of your skin.

Ingredients:
  Optional: 6 fresh rose petals
  2 tbsps rosewater (you can pick this up at a natural food store)
  1 tbsp natural yogurt, room temperature
  1 tbsp warm honey (Just zap it in the microwave for a few seconds)

Preparation:
Soak rose petals, and then crush them in a bowl.
Add the rosewater, yogurt and honey.
Mix well and apply to the skin.
Leave on for 10 minutes.
Rinse.

Hair Care

We've covered washing and conditioning – that's a given by now. Do take the time each morning to style your hair. Styling your hair doesn't have to take a long time – ask your parents to take you to a salon for a good cut and style. This will help speed up your daily routine, plus it makes you feel like a million bucks!

If your hair is thick and course, deep condition once a week.

No matter the brand you chose, make sure you're using a shampoo and conditioner designed for your hair type (fine, thick, wavy, etc.)

Nail Care

As a First Style Fashionista, your nails should be cut shorter than those of, say, your college-aged sister. Fingernails and toenails should be cleaned daily and filed regularly. Nail polish is okay, but again age is a factor: keep it light (beiges, pinks, etc.) Save the reds and darker tones for when you're older. No chipped polish, either – your overall style will suffer!

First Style Tips:
Do It Yourself Mani and Pedi!

Manicure

Remove old polish. To get rid of polish around your cuticle, use the tip of an orangewood stick (this is a skinny stick available in any drugstore) wrapped in cotton and soaked in nail polish remover. If nails are too long, trim them evenly to match one another.

Sweep a file from side to side in one direction.

To clean any dirt or remaining polish, and to soften cuticles, fill a small bowl with warm water and a mild liquid soap, then soak your fingernails for a few minutes.

Rub a good amount of lotion into your cuticles. This will help you to push them back without damaging them.

Use a cuticle pusher to nudge cuticles off the nail plate, and then wipe the surface with a clean towel. It's best not to cut cuticles.

Apply a clear base coat – this helps polish stick to the nail. Once it's dry, brush on one to two coats of polish. Start with a stroke down the center of the nail, then add polish on each side. Finish with a topcoat, and don't do anything until they're completely dry!

Pedicure

Remove old polish (same technique used for a manicure).

Use clippers to cut toenails straight across (cutting down the sides of the nail can cause ingrown toenails). Don't allow nails to extend past the tip of the toe.

Smooth the nail edge with a file, working in one direction.

Rub a good amount of lotion into cuticles, and then soak your feet in sudsy water (a large bowl works for this).

Massage lotion onto your feet

Gently push back cuticles with an orangewood stick then dry your feet. Apply a base coat, and then follow with one or two coats of polish (follow the three stroke method you use on your manicure). Remember to add the topcoat, and refrain from putting your shoes on until the polish is completely dry!

Beauty Log:
Sometimes it's helpful to write down when you did what. For example:

Date of last hair cut:
Date of last facial:
Date of last manicure:
Date of last pedicure:

Remember, the way you present yourself to the world tells the world an awful lot about you. If you want to be thought of as a stylish, sophisticated young lady, you must take care to display yourself as such. That's what **First Style Fashionistas** are all about!

Duexemi Partie: Easy Etiquette!

"Respect for right conduct is felt by everybody".
- Jane Austen

First impressions are lasting impressions. It's an old cliché, but oh-so-true. You may have your look down, but your words and actions are the things people will most remember about you.

Manners matter....but do they matter to you?

1. During a family dinner, you...

a. Sit up straight with your napkin in your lap, and ask, "Please pass the...." when you'd like something.

b. Never speak with your mouth full, but sometimes reach across someone when you want something

c. Get mad at Mom for telling you to get your elbows off the table and to stop texting

d. I don't eat with my family – are you crazy! I grab my plate and head for my room!

2. When meeting someone for the first time, you always...

a. Extend your hand and say, "It's very nice to meet you."

b. Offer a polite 'hello' and a smile

c. Sort of mumble 'hi'. It's so hard to talk to strangers!

d. If they're lucky, they'll get a nod from you before you quickly dash off to meet people you're more interested in.

3. In a public place, you...

a. Always keep your voice low

b. Lower your voice after someone's given you a dirty look

c. Have a tendency to walk too fast and yell back   and forth with your friends

d. Were once asked to leave for being too loud and acting too crazy!

4. When it comes to chewing gum, you...

a. Rarely do it

b. Do it, but try to remember not to smack or blow bubbles

c. Wonder why it's such a bit deal not to smack–everybody does it, right?

d. Once ended up in detention for not only violating the school's gum policy, but for actually   sticking your used gum underneath your desk.

5. In the company of adults, you...

a. Are always on your best behavior

b. Are polite, but quickly make an excuse to get away from them

c. Rarely speak or make eye contact

d. Make a run for it! Who wants to hang out with the grown-ups?

6. The new girl in school seems really weird, so you...

a. Make an effort to at least say 'hi' to her

b. Smile in her direction

c. Avoid her

d. Relate her weirdness to everyone on Facebook.

Mostly A's:
You realize that First Style Fashionistas understand the concept of the 'whole package'. It doesn't matter how great you look, if you don't act great, you'll lose major style points.

Mostly B's:
You do make an effort, but it's so hard sometimes to remember all the rules!

Mostly C's:
You are aware of the rules, but just aren't that interested in following them. It can be fun to misbehave!

Mostly D's:
You have a 'take me as I am' attitude. It's great to be your own person, but you're running the risk of becoming a person no one wants to be around.

It's one thing to look fabulous; however, if you're not behaving fabulously then you'll kill your style potential. Don't roll your eyes at me, young lady.

Take a cue from these girl...

Meet and Greet

Excited doesn't even begin to describe Bianca! She's in 8th grade now, and hopes St. Francis High School, the most exclusive private high school in town, accepts her. She's completed her paper work, her teachers have written letters of recommendation for her, so now all she has to do is ace the interview with Sister Margret, the headmistress of the school.

"Bianca, it's a pleasure to meet you," Sister Margret begins. As she extends her hand to Bianca, Bianca just keeps on walking, right into the sister's office.

"Hi, Sister. How ya doin'?" asks Bianca as she plops down in the chair in front of Sister Margret's desk. She crosses her legs, Indian-style, on the chair, her skirt barely containing her.

"I'm well, thank you. Tell me a bit about yourself." Sister Margret eyes Bianca very carefully, a hint of disapproval upon her face.

"Not much to tell, really," Bianca begins, smacking her gum. "My grades are good, I'm a cheerleader, and I know I'd be a great student here. St. Francis is the awesomest!" Bianca continues to babble while Sister Margret takes notes.

Two weeks later, Bianca receives a letter telling her she was not accepted into St. Francis.

Did her first impression hinder her chances? Most likely. You see, looking good on paper (report cards, transcripts, recommendation letters) won't do you any good if you don't represent yourself well.

Let's try again, Bianca:

"Bianca, it's a pleasure to meet you," Sister Margret begins. As she extends her hand to Bianca, Bianca takes it and looks Sister Margret in the eye.

"It's a pleasure to meet you, Sister Margret. Thank you so much for taking the time to visit with me," Bianca says.

She then waits for Sister Margret to invite her into her office. Bianca follows the sister inside, but doesn't sit down until she's asked to do so.

She sits quietly, her knees together and ankles crossed, and waits for Sister Margret to begin.

"Tell me a bit about yourself and why you want to attend our school," Sister Margret says with a smile.

"Yes, ma'am. Although I make good grades, they don't always come easily. I work really hard. I've been involved in student council and was a cheerleader this year. I'd love to attend St. Francis because I believe it's the best academically and it's well-rounded. There is so much for students to do, and I think that's wonderful!"

Following the interview, Bianca stands and once again looks Sister Margret in the eye and shakes her hand. "Thank you so much, ma'am, for taking the time to talk with me," she says.

Bianca handled herself maturely and used her best manners (hand shake, eye contact, sitting correctly, answering concisely rather than babbling). Two weeks later, she received word that she had been accepted to St. Francis.

The first impression we make lasts for a very long time. That's why it's so important to be courteous, to listen, to display our best posture, and to maintain eye contact. We must never ramble on about ourselves, and we must use correct grammar (yes, your English class is important, so pay attention!). Gum chewing is a definite no-no.

Dinner Dilemma

Debbie comes from a casual family. Dinner is usually take-out eaten in front of the television. Debbie's a little worried, though; her 8th grade banquet is coming up soon, and she has no idea how to eat properly at the table. She's too embarrassed to ask her friends, and she knows her family will be no help.

Luckily, her homeroom teacher, sensing Debbie was a bit nervous about the banquet, pulled her aside and handed her a slip of paper. It read:

The Supper Method

Sit up
Use proper utensils
Place setting looks like this:

Place napkin in lap, and elbows off the table
Eat slowly and with your mouth closed.
Reaching is a no-no.

An excited Debbie ran home and showed her mom. Mom realized she'd really let Debbie down in this department, and decided that they'd start applying the Supper Method that very evening. It worked. Debbie got the confidence she needed before the banquet, and the whole family now sits down to a proper, well-mannered meal every night!

Phone Niceties and No-no's:

Nicety:
Answering the family phone with "Hello, this is the Miller residence. How may I help you?"

No-no:
Answering the family phone any other way than the example above.

Nicety:
Taking messages for family members and then repeating the message back to the caller to make sure you got it right.

No-no:
"My mom's not here!" followed by a slamming down of the phone.

Nicety:
Your friend's dad answers your friend's phone. "Hello, Mr. Miller. This is Sheila. May I speak to Beth?" is the proper way to get the ball rolling here.

No-no:
Your friend's dad answers your friend's phone. "Dude! I need to talk to Beth right now!" Never address an adult with anything but Mr. or Ms. unless told to do so by the adult. Never demand an adult do something for you. A little nicety goes a long way with grown-ups!

Nicety:
Ignoring your cell phone during family time (this includes dinner and outings). Heck, turn it off if you need to!

No-no:
Spending time texting or talking while in the company of your family – or anyone, for that matter.

Netiquette

Just a few years ago, the Internet didn't exist – can you believe that?! Now with just a touch of a button, we can research any topic and stay in touch with our friends through email and networking sites, such as Facebook. There are some rules here, though, that were primarily developed to keep you safe, so take note:

Never list your phone number or address on any networking site. There are many dangerous people out there. It's best to keep your pages set to private for this reason.

Never post photos or videos of yourself or of your friends doing something you wouldn't want your parents to see.

A First Style Fashionista NEVER posts nasty things about another person on the Internet. This is called cyber-bullying. It could be considered slander, therefore making it illegal. You or your parents could be prosecuted for something like this.

Public and private schools can access what you've been up to on the Internet. Most are taking strong measures to insure cyber-bullying does not occur by enforcing suspensions and expulsions. College admission boards and future employers can also see what you've been up to. Lack of netiquette can and will keep you out of that school you've been dying to get into or keep you from landing a great job. Be smart!

All the World's a Stage

Tiffany loves to perform. She sings, dances, cheers – you name it, she does it. The problem is that Tiffany will burst into song at any given moment. She's also been known to dance her way to her math class each day. Because she's had some voice training, she knows how to project her voice, and as a result she's REALLY LOUD! Her teachers are constantly telling her to lower her voice. Once, during a field trip to the museum, someone complained about Tiffany's boisterous behavior and the whole class ended up in trouble. In all honesty, she's starting to get on her friends' nerves.

First Style Fashionistas always play to their strengths. It's great that Tiffany loves what she does, but Tiffany needs to realize that there's a time and place for everything. Perform on the stage, cheer on the field, but keep that stuff out of the classroom and other public places. Also, focus on keeping your voice down in public; strangers don't want to know what you're talking about.

Going, Going, Gone!

Nahla always seems to be in a hurry. She sprints, jogs, and trots everywhere! She's constantly bumping into people, and is usually called out by her teachers for running in the hall.

Nahla needs to understand that one thing that will kill a girl's style is the way in which she carries herself. A First Style Fashionista walks at a regular pace, with her head held high and her shoulders back. She goes to extreme measures to insure that she gives everyone around her their space. She's graceful and elegant, and those are two traits that will carry her very far in life!

Girl, Interrupted

Olivia, outgoing social butterfly that she is, invited the new girl in school, Annie, to sit with her at lunch one day. Thrilled, Annie followed Olivia to the table; it's so hard being the new girl.

"So," Olivia began, "what classes are you taking this semester? Oh, my gosh, you don't have mean old Mr. Hand, do you? He's the worst! You'll like Mrs. O'Kelly, though; she's so sweet and gives us extra time on assignments if we need it. Did you say you had history with Mr. Hand?"

"No," Annie began, thinking to herself that she hadn't been given a chance to say anything, "I have Miss..."

"Oh, my gosh, have you met Josh? He's the hottest boy in school. I like him so much! Do you think he likes me?" Olivia asked.

"I don't know Josh..." but before Annie could continue, Olivia interrupted one more time.

"Oh, and stay away from Becky. She's trouble. She said some really bad things about me last year. And another thing..."

Poor Annie felt trapped. Not only could she not get a word in edgewise, she felt really uncomfortable hearing things about people whom she hadn't met yet. Annie decided not to sit with Olivia anymore.

It's great that Olivia invited Annie to sit with her during lunch, and it's great that she wanted to share some things about some of her fellow students and teachers with Annie. Unfortunately, Olivia went about this the wrong way. Dominating a conversation or interrupting people is not only a turn-off, it's just plain rude! We make more friends by asking sincere questions and LISTENING than we do by simply running our mouths.

The Golden Rule

Do unto others as you'd have them do unto you. In other words, treat everyone with kindness and respect. They, in turn, will treat you kindly and respectfully!

Troisieme Partie: Well, Well, Well!

"Every human being is the author of his own health or disease."
-Buddha

We can't look or act our best if we don't feel our best. So, answer honestly: how are you?

1. When it comes to eating healthy, you...

a. Find it's quite easy. You like your fruits and veggies

b. Try to eat a salad or a piece of fruit a few times a week

c. Eat your veggies, but only under protest

d. Does pizza three times a day count as healthy eating?

2. Still on the subject of eating, you...

a. Do your best to eat three healthy meals a day

b. Eat a couple of times a day – you're trying to lose some weight

c. Skip meals altogether and just snack

d. You don't like it, and have resorted to some pretty secretive measures to keep your family and friends from knowing just how little food you're actually taking in.

3. Generally, you...

a. Are outgoing and usually feel good about yourself

b. Are comfortable with yourself and enjoy the company of a few close friends

c. Would like to make more friends, but you're kind of shy and not sure how

d. Are a loner, for reasons you'd just as soon not get into.

4. Anytime you have a problem, you know you can easily talk to...

a. Mom or Dad

b. A trusted adult (an aunt or teacher)

c. Your best friend

d. No one

5. You realize that exercise is...

a. Very important, and do it on a regular basis

b. Important, but you don't do it regularly

c. A pain!

d. Unnecessary – why bother?!

6. You take the time every day to...

a. Pray or meditate

b. Sit and think

c. Write in a journal

d. Yell at people when you don't get your way.

Mostly A's:
You realize that your health is a gift and you must care for it properly. Same goes for your mind.

Mostly B's:
You know that staying well both physically and mentally is important, and you do it.....sometimes.

Mostly C's:
You'd like to feel better, but you're not quite sure where to start.

Mostly D's:
You may be more concerned with the outward rather than the inward. You've taken some pretty drastic steps in order to get what you want.

You've got the right outfit, your head is held high, but there's something that just isn't working. Are you tired? Stressed? Hungry? No one, no matter her age, can truly be stylish if she's not well. That's why it's even more important that we devote caring for the inside as much as we do the outside.

Let's begin...

You Are What You Eat

Ashley wouldn't eat a vegetable if her life depended on it. A sip of water? Forget it; she reaches for soda when she's thirsty. On most days, breakfast is a donut...or two...or three. Lunch is whatever she gets from the school vending machine, and dinner is whatever the pizza place delivers that day.

Ashley's tired and cranky a lot of the time. Her clothes seem to be getting smaller and smaller, and her skin is starting to resemble some of that pizza she's so fond of. She can't do anything with her hair, either – it's so dull and lifeless – and that only makes her even crankier.

What's a girl to do?

It's easy: Eat correctly, drink water, and enjoy that junk food on a limited (once or twice a week) basis.

Fact: Fresh vegetables and fruits will improve our skin, the quality of our hair, and our mood. They'll also help us maintain a healthy weight. Do it right by eating at least five servings of fruits and veggies every day.

Fact: Nothing is better for you than a glass of water. Sure, it doesn't have the fizzy fun taste of soda or the sugary goodness of some juices, but it really is the best for our skin, hair, energy, and mental clarity. Many people depend on sodas for an energy boost, and they'll get it; however, it's short-lived and comes to a screeching halt, leaving us tired and unable to focus.

Fact: As long as you eat healthy most of the time, it's okay to eat an occasional cookie or indulge in a slice of pizza. Everything in moderation – that's the key!

Magnificent Munchies:

Snack mix
Fruit salad
A banana with peanut butter
An apple with a slice of cheese

Water Works

Jazz up that glass of water by adding a slice of lemon or lime. Crystal Light is a great and low calorie source to add pizzazz to H2O.

Quiet Conundrum

Serena feels low. Terribly shy, she finds it difficult to make friends. She sits alone in the cafeteria during lunch, and rarely utters a word throughout the day.

Her dad works a lot, so he's not home much. Her mom is ill most days, and spends a great amount of time in her room. When Mom's not ill, she simply ignores Serena or yells at her for not keeping her room clean, getting a bad grade, eating junk food, etc. Serena is an only child who feels she has nowhere to turn when the times get really tough during her lonely days.

Serena dreams of becoming an artist, but figures she's just not talented enough to make it happen. She'd love to enter some of her school's art contests, but she's afraid the other students will laugh at her work.

If only she had someone to talk to, and some way to sort out her feelings.

But how...and who?

School Counselor

Serena's best bet would be to make an appointment with her school counselor or a trusted teacher to discuss her situation at home. Because she has little self-esteem, she needs some adult guidance to help her deal with her problems at home. This will help her as she battles her shyness.

Church or Youth Organization

Serena needs to get involved with people her own age. Given her shyness, a church or community youth organization might be more accepting and welcoming of Serena and help her overcome her fears. Social interaction is necessary, but it can be scary if you're like Serena. The adults involved in these organizations can offer the guidance Serena is not getting from home at the moment.

Safe Online Networks

Interacting with someone online might make it easier for Serena to interact with someone in person; however, it's important to find forums that are safe for young people. Serena might enlist the help of her school counselor or librarian to steer her in the right direction.

A Note: It's vital that you are extremely careful about the sites you choose, and the information you put on those sites (go back and review what we discussed in Netiquette)

Model Behavior

Nicole dreams of becoming a fashion model. She studies the pictures in every magazine out there, hoping that her dream will come true some day. She realizes models are super-thin, so she skips breakfast... and lunch... and sometimes will only eat a few carrot sticks for dinner. Nicole finds it hard to concentrate in school, and it's all she can do to make it through her gym class. Her parents and teachers are concerned, but she merely tells them she isn't hungry.

There are times she eats more than she thinks she should, so she sticks her finger down her throat and forces herself to throw up. She read somewhere that taking laxatives will also help keep one's weight down. She's on her way to the drugstore to pick up a box.

Obviously, Nicole has developed some seriously scary health patterns. There are some things Nicole needs to realize:

Her health is far more important than looking like a model. Many models are terribly unhealthy. Refusing to eat not only causes fatigue; it could cause one's hair to fall out. Vitamin deficiency will result, which will take its toll on her bones, her nails, and her skin.

Another thing Nicole must come to understand is that in real life models don't look the way they do in magazines. Computers can change shapes, eye color, and hair color – all of it. What Nicole sees in the magazines isn't real.

Terms to know:

Anorexia is a loss of the desire to eat. The term can be used medically as a symptom of many illnesses. It is more commonly used to describe a psychological disorder of self-induced starvation in an effort to become thin. (www.nutritionworks.net/glossary)

Bulimia is a disorder characterized by bingeing (episodes of eating large amounts of food) and purging (getting rid of the food by vomiting or using laxatives). (www.dietscam.org/basic/glossary)

If you feel as if you might be suffering from anorexia or bulimia, seek help immediately. Tell an adult and visit your doctor. If you fear a friend may be suffering from an eating disorder, tell a trusted adult (parent, school counselor, school nurse, etc.) Anorexia and bulimia are extremely dangerous and life-threatening conditions.

Ssshhh... Quiet, Please...

With our crazy, hectic lives, it's easy for girls to get overwhelmed from time to time. In order to keep our sanity, First Style Fashionistas take a little time each day to do any – or all- of the following:

Journal writing – getting the stuff out of your head and on paper really helps sort things out. Keep your journal private. Remember, your journal and your online blog are two completely different things!

Meditation or prayer -just sitting and being is relaxing in and of itself. Close your eyes and focus on something pleasant and take a deep breath. You'll find your thoughts clear up in no time. Appealing to a higher power and having faith that all will work out exactly as it should (not necessarily the way you want it to) gets so many people through the day.

An attitude of gratitude – sure, life isn't fabulous all the time, but you'll find if you give thanks for what you've got, more good things will come to you.

La Quatrieme Partie: Success Strategies

"I have so many goals."
-Tyra Banks

It's awesome to have your look, your health, and your overall well-being in place. Now, it's time to think about your overall success – in school, and in life. It's one thing to look fabulous...quite another to feel fabulous...and by striving toward your personal best each day, you'll accomplish many amazing things now and in the future! Check out what these girls are up to...

Who's Responsible?

Nothing ever seems to go right for Rita. Her mom dropped her off at school late (because Rita overslept), she didn't complete her homework (because she was too busy watching TV last night) and her new shirt is missing a button (because she didn't check it the night before to make sure it was ready to wear). "It's all Mom's fault!" Rita exclaims to her friends. "Nothing ever goes right for me. Sometimes I think people are just out to get me!"

Rita needs to understand this: she is at an age in which she should become responsible for a lot that goes on in her life. It's not fair for her to blame her mom, her family, her teachers, or anyone else when things don't go right. No one is entitled to anything in this world; if we want great things to happen, we must go out there and make them happen. Like Rita, we are responsible for our actions, and must face the consequences of those actions.

You've Got to Believe

Maggie wants to be a writer someday. She's afraid to tell her friends or family because she fears they might make fun of her. Her grades in English really aren't that great, but she loves reading and she loves to write stories. She's got tons of ideas and half-hearted attempts written down in notebooks, but she isn't quite sure how to make it happen.

The best thing Maggie can do is to develop the confidence she needs in order to succeed. She needs to tell someone (her parents, her teacher, etc.) about her dreams. Then, she needs to keep working on her writing. She could enter contests, and even try to have something published. She needs to believe in herself and in her talents. If she doesn't, who will?

Goal Power

Gloria has one thing on her mind: to make the varsity soccer team next year. She lives for soccer; she practices every day, watches every tournament she can, and reads as much about the game as possible. Gloria also writes down her progress each week in order to see how far she's come – and how far she needs to go. She knows that learning the strategies, and getting out there and playing the game, will help her reach her goal (no pun intended!)

Gloria's doing it exactly right! When we have a goal in mind, we must work toward that goal every day. It's called 'keeping our eye on the prize'. Things don't just automatically happen – we have to go out there and make them happen. Gloria's wise to write down her goal, and to chart her weekly progress. She's specific with her goal, too: making the varsity team. When we know exactly what we want, we'll have a greater chance of getting there.

Fake It 'Til You Make It

Charlie struggles in the confidence department. She's the tallest girl in her class, and oftentimes she's just so shy it's hard for her to talk to anyone. She's taking a drama class this year, and the teacher offered her some very good advice during one of their character studies. The teacher told Charlie and the rest of the class, "Decide what you want your character to be, and then just be the character." Charlie's thinking that perhaps she'll try that theory off the stage, too.

Charlie's absolutely right! It's hard knowing what to do or say sometimes. Heck, it's hard to know who we want to be, too! The drama teacher's advice was great; one of the best success strategies out there is to act as if you're already the person you want to be. Now be careful, though – this won't work if you're trying to be someone else. Stay true to yourself. If you want others to see you as kind and confident, then 'play the role' of a kind and confident person. This means thinking like, talking like, dressing like, and acting like the person you want to be.

Successful Surroundings

Stacey's having a rough time of things lately. Her friends at school seem to always be in trouble – they talk too much, pick on the younger kids, and make huge messes in the cafeteria. She knows the other kids and even the teachers don't like their group, and as a result, they don't like Stacey. She's never causing any of the trouble; she's just always with the group when they're stirring things up. Stacey knows she needs to make some changes, but she's not sure how to go about making them. Even bad friends are better than no friends at all, right?

Wrong. Stacey must separate herself from these trouble-makers immediately. Their bad reputation is rubbing off on her – even though she's not part of the problem, her association with them leads others to believe that she is. Stacey needs to find some friends who are positive and who are active within the school community. There is safety in numbers, so Stacey shouldn't fear that her old friends might retaliate against her. If she builds a positive force of good friends around her, she'll be just fine!

What it boils down to is this: in order to be a true First Style Fashionista, you must commit yourself to becoming a 'class act'. A class act is someone who sets high standards for herself, and works hard to live up to those standards.

She is an excellent role model for her peers, and maintains her dignity, even during those tough times.

She avoids 'mean girl' behavior.

She takes responsibility for her actions and for the results of those actions.

She constantly strives to make life better for herself and for those around her.

She understands that the habits she develops now will most likely be the habits she carries into adulthood.

She is, in a nutshell, fabulous!

Okay, now that you've got some insight into what a First Style Fashionista is all about, let's see if you've made some changes!

1. I knew all along that...

a. Fashion, good manners, and good habits go hand-in hand and I'll do my best to live my best each day!

b. That I needed some help in certain areas, and I'm glad I finally got it!

c. Style is important, but I'm not sure if I'm willing just yet to make the effort

d. I'm a mess, and I'm proud of it!

2. I'm really excited about...

a. Shopping for new clothes and strutting my stylish stuff!

b. Showing off my new table manners

c. Taking tiny steps toward being fabulous. My friends would give me a hard time if I tried it all at once.

d. Eating a whole box of donuts!

3. When I get older I want to be...

a. Fabulous!

b. Considered a nice person

c. Left alone

d. Who wants to get older? I'm having fun now!

4. When it comes to setting a positive example for other girls, I'm...

a. Doing it now!

b. Ready!

c. Almost ready!

d. Are you kidding me?

5.When things get rough, I realize I must...

a. Seek help immediately from someone I trust

b. Think about it carefully

c. Think about talking to someone

d. Ignore it

6. You will always find me...

a. Looking my best, showing kindness and respect to others, and remaining focused on the things that really matter

b. Trying to do the right thing

c. Thinking about doing the right thing

d. Not doing anything!

Mostly A's:
Congratulations! You are officially a First Style Fashionista! Your job now is to help others reach their full potential by setting a positive example, assisting them when they're in need, and offering little bits of kindness throughout the day (a smile, a warm hello, etc.)

Mostly B's:
You're well on your way to becoming a First Style Fashionista! You know what it takes, but you might need just a gentle nudge to get you there. Consider this your nudge and make it happen for yourself!

Mostly C's:
You get it, but aren't quite sure if you're ready for it. That's okay. At the very least, I want you to think seriously about what we've discussed. With time, you'll come to realize what it takes, exactly, to be a First Style Fashionista – you're just this close – so take my hand and let's do it together!

Mostly D's:
You, my lovely, need to review what we've discussed, and to realize this: Many times, our 'devil-may-care' act is merely that – at act. Deep down, you know you've got the potential, but for whatever reason (lack of confidence, fear of failure, etc.) you've yet to take those steps toward fabulosity. Take that first step with me now. Trust me – you won't regret it!

Et enfin...

So there you have it, my darlings. Becoming a First Style Fashionista is more than fashion (although our clothing choices are VERY important!). It's about the words we speak, the thoughts we think, and our actions.

It's about striving to be our absolute best in everything we do. It's about contributing to our community in a positive way. It's about remaining true to ourselves, and treating ourselves with the utmost respect. It's about respecting the rights of others, including those pesky younger siblings and boring old teachers!

The habits you develop now are most likely the ones you will take with you as you grow into an adult. Experts tell us that it takes three weeks to develop a habit, so here's my challenge for you: see how much you can accomplish these next three weeks by focusing on the type of young woman you want to become. Write down your goals in a notebook or journal, and review them every day. Visualize yourself as being successful in every part of your life. Take action each day to help you reach your goals. And never give up!

Life is meant to be lived happily, successfully, and fabulously! All it takes is respect and responsibility... and a great pair of shoes!

If you have any questions about First Style, please email:

beth@newmanimage.com

Or visit:

www.newmanimage.info

Miss Beth also offers online tutorials for First Style Fashionistas everywhere in the areas of fashion, etiquette, wellness, study skills, and success strategies.

She also invites you to become a First Style Fashionista on Facebook!

A First Style Fashionista's 52 Weeks of Fabulosity!

This is your journal. You can write whatever you want on the following pages. Jot down your goals, reflect on any challenges you may be facing, plan your wardrobe....this is your own little handbook to help you as you travel the road to fabulosity!

Week 1

"A girl should be two things: classy and fabulous."
-Coco Chanel

Week 2

"If you think you can, you can. If you think you can't, you're right."
-Mary Kay Ash

Week 3

"Far away there in the sunshine are my highest aspirations. I may not reach them, but I can look up and see their beauty, believe in them, and try to follow where they lead."
-Louisa May Alcott

Week 4
"Don't compromise yourself. You are all you've got."
-Janis Joplin

Week 5

"Remember no one can make you feel inferior without your consent."
-Eleanor Roosevelt

Week 6

*"Do not follow where the path may lead.
Go instead where there is no path and leave a trail."*
-Harold R. McAlindon

Week 7

"We are what we repeatedly do. Excellence therefore, is not an act but a habit."
-Aristotle

Week 8

"Nothing contributes so much to tranquilize the mind as a steady purpose."
-Mary Shelley

Week 9
"The more a man knows, the more he forgives."
-Catherine the Great

Week 10

"A loving heart is the truest wisdom."
-Charles Dickens

Week 11

"Living a life is like constructing a building: if you start wrong, you'll end wrong."
-Maya Angelou

Week 12

"When we do the best that we can, we never know what miracle is wrought in our life, or in the life of another."
-Helen Keller

Week 13

"Your future is created by what you do today, not tomorrow."
-Robert Kiyosaki

Week 14

"Everyone is here because he or she has a place to fill..."
-Deepak Chopra

Week 15

"The secret is to decide that you're beautiful already...once you do, other people will believe it, too."
-Victoria Moran

Week 16

"A beautiful gesture is really a very rare thing."
-Jacqueline Kenney Onassis

Week 17
"There's always time to rewrite your own script."
-Janice Dickinson

Week 18

"People are just as happy as they make up their minds to be."
-Abraham Lincoln

Week 19

"All our dreams can come true – if we have the courage to pursue them."
-Walt Disney

Week 20

"I believe that every woman has the seeds of charm within her. She has only to learn to liberate it."
-Eileen Ashcroft

Week 21

"To accomplish great things, we must not only act, but also dream, not only plan, but also believe."
-Anatole France

Week 22

"Every thought we think is creating our future."
-Louise L. Hay

Week 23
"Make it work!"
-Tim Gunn

Week 24

"Aim not for what you are, but for what you could be."

-Lucas Hellmer

Week 25

"This world is but a canvas to our imaginations."
-Henry David Thoreau

Week 26

"For beautiful eyes, look for the good in others; for beautiful lips, speak only words of kindness; and for poise, walk with the knowledge that you are never alone."
-Audrey Hepburn

Week 27

"Fashion is very important. It is life-enhancing and, like everything that gives pleasure, it is worth doing well."

-Vivienne Westwood

Week 28

"Despite everything, I believe that people are really good at heart."

-Anne Frank

Week 29

"The biggest adventure you can ever take is to live the life of your dreams."
-Oprah Winfrey

Week 30

"Faith is taking the first step even when you don't see the whole staircase."
-Martin Luther King, Jr.

Week 31

"It isn't where you came from; it's where you're going that counts."
-Ella Fitzgerald

Week 32

"A dream you dream alone is only a dream. A dream you dream together is reality."
-John Lennon

Week 33
"We can overcome evil with greater good."
-Laura Bush

Week 34

"Attitude is everything."
-Diane von Furstenberg

Week 35

"Try not. Do or do not. There is no try."
-Yoda

Week 36

"Always turn a negative situation into a positive situation."
-Michael Jordan

Week 37

"You'll never do a whole lot unless you're brave enough to try."
-Dolly Parton

Week 38

"It takes a great deal of bravery to stand up to our friends, but just as much to stand up to our enemies."
-J. K. Rowling

Week 39

"I like to dream, but I like to make things happen."
-Heidi Klum

Week 40

*"Never forget where you came from, and reach back
to help someone else come forward, too."*
-Alpha Alexander

Week 41

"To thine own self be true."
-William Shakespeare

Week 42

"Find something that you're really interested in doing in your life. Pursue it, set goals and commit yourself to excellence. Do the best you can."
-Chris Evert

Week 43

"Education is the key to unlock the golden door of freedom."
-George Washington Carver

Week 44

"The only real elegance comes from the mind; if you've got that, the rest really comes from it."
-Diana Vreeland

Week 45

"Beauty of style and harmony and grace and good rhythm depend on simplicity."
-Plato

Week 46

"A truly elegant taste is generally accompanied by excellence of heart."
-Henry Fielding

Week 47

"To me, you can't have style without being inspired."
-Isaac Mizrahi

Week 48

"You can't cross a sea by merely staring at the water."
-Rabindranath Tagore

Week 49

"You have to be careful out in the world. It's so easy to get turned."
-Elvis Presley

Week 50

"*Efforts and courage are not enough without purpose and direction.*"
-John F. Kennedy

Week 51

"Why...wouldn't you want to be one of the fabulous people, the life-enhancers?"
-Simon Doonan

Week 52

"A journey of 1,000 miles must begin with one step."
-Chinese Proverb